THE RIM BENDERS

POEMS AND DISCOURSES

FLORIDA POETRY SERIES

Books by Lola Haskins

Desire Lines, New and Selected Poems, 2001

Extranjera, 1998

Visions of Florida, 1994
with photographs by Woody Walters

Forty-four Ambitions for the Piano, 1994

Hunger, 1993

Castings, 1984

Planting the Children, 1983

Chapbooks

A Lifetime from Any Land We Knew, 1998

Across Her Broad Lap Something Wonderful, 1989

THE RIM BENDERS

POEMS AND DISCOURSES

Lola Haskins

Anhinga Press, 2001
Tallahassee, Florida

Cover Art – *Thinking About the Past*, Maggie Taylor

Author Photo – Gerald Haskins

Cover design, book design, and production – Lynne Knight

Typeset in Bitstream Arrus and Adobe Slimbach.

Library of Congress Cataloging-in-Publication Data
The Rim Benders: Poems and Discourses by Lola Haskins – First Edition
ISBN 0938078-70-4
Library of Congress Card Number: 2001091692

*This publication is sponsored in part by a grant from the Florida Department
of State, Division of Cultural Affairs, and the Florida Arts Council.*

Anhinga Press Inc. is a nonprofit corporation dedicated wholly
to the publication and appreciation of fine poetry.
For personal orders, catalogs and information write to:
Anhinga Press
P.O. Box 10595
Tallahassee, FL 32302
Web site: www.anhinga.org
E-mail: info@anhinga.org

Published in the United States by Anhinga Press, Tallahassee, Florida.
First Edition, 2001

Printed by QUESTprint, Orlando, Florida.

For Ger

Contents

Acknowledgments

Some of the poems in this book first appeared in *Artful Dodge,
Beloit Poetry Journal, Cantilever, Caprice, Clay Palm Review,
Crazyhorse, Cream City Review, Flyway, Free Lunch, Georgia
Review, The Little Magazine, Lowell Review, New York Quarterly,
Octavo, Organica, Passages North, Prairie Schooner, River City,
Sojourner, Southern Review, Tampa Review, Third Muse,
This is Not Art, West Branch,* and *The Writer's Quill.*

"Tuning" won the 1994 Emily Dickinson Prize from the Poetry
Society of America.

"The Shoes" and "Message #2" are anthologized in *Best of
Sojourner,* University of Iowa Press, 1999

The cover image, *Thinking About the Past* by Maggie Taylor, is
used with kind permission of the artist.

THE RIM BENDERS

The Rim Benders

Perhaps the most critical moment in the construction of a
grand piano is that in which the strip of wood which will
be the final casing of the instrument must be matched to
the curve of the frame.

They have twelve minutes to marry
the thin edge to its curve.
There is great pressure. Fine wood
does not wish to bend. Let us
lean with them into this poem.

And if we fail, the set glue
leaves gaps, sharp mistakes
of air we will always see.
But how can we not try? These are
the twelve minutes of our lives.

ONE

Winnowing the True

Imitation pearls drawn across the teeth
feel smooth. Dyed fur resists when blown.
When out for butter, shun bright yellow.

A knot that moves on its branch is not a knot.
A word thrown over the shoulder is not a discussion.
A brick is not a personal flotation device.

A father will cover his sleeping son
but leave his dreams alone.
A jeweler will cut the extra face and risk the gem.
A Master will tell you he plays, a little.

The Humper

for A Z

He can carry it by himself up your stairs.
Such a load of music would break you.
You stand aside. You think what a risk
it would be, even to follow him.

You note his cheeks, smooth as lemoned
wood, his taut veins, and, in his arms
your piano's dumbstruck shine. You know
you cannot hope to match his touch.

Chewing the Soup

It is how he did not die.
Fifty chews, then seventy-five,
then more. It is what kept
his sharpened ribs from breaking
skin. It is why, when freed,
he alone could stand.

He tells us how difficult it was,
how soon the starving throat
craves to swallow. Failing soup,
he would chew his own saliva.
Only the poets in the audience
are not surprised.

The Field

The field snatches at my ankles like a cat.
How can I not stroke it,
seeing how it purrs with bees.

All day, all night, the nuzzling goes on.
Each lipped stroke's a small rip.
The young field mends and mends.

The field has lain so long in its bath of sky
it forgets who it is, how it used to rise
and comb its hair.

The field is never left alone.
Finally its high bones become so clear
it is beautiful only in photographs.

Florida

In Florida, when the forty-foot limo slows,
Mickey Mouse gets out.

But take a canoe on the New in March
and see the swamp azaleas

mirroring their pink clusters on the water.
See how turtles plop from logs

as you pass. See the heavy alligator enter.
He is somewhere under your boat.

Sand sculptures rise in a Daytona parking lot.
Elvis and The Last Supper. Snow White

and Moses. With proper care these may last,
the card says, months.

In parts of Jacksonville, there are people
who cannot breathe.

We think we're mermaids. We think blue-organdied
maidens waterskied. We think

we can dump shit in the sea forever.
When it rains in Florida,

it rains from the heart.

Elegy on a Winter Morning

To the little fires burning under bridges
To the newspapers stuffed in shirts —
the front page facing a nipple,
the Thanksgiving parade that ends
in a thicket of chest hair,
the father who lifts his son towards a throat —

To the hands spread over fires
the hands with their shining veins
To the way they gathered with such patience
anything that might burn
To the way the fingers of men
who do not know each other, almost touch.

Meteor Shower

Angels whirling in the ballroom
of the sky
Angels in their long white gloves
Their shiny
hair swirls Their pale skirts glow
But one has
no partner One stands alone hurling
chunks of
rock and blue fire and deep into
the earth
that angel's name burns.

On Poetry

I slow, crossing the street,
          to give the speeding car a chance
at the bright jut inside my leg,
      startling
as the blind eyes
         of the albino who suddenly
turns,
      a chance at skid — that acrid rubber
stench.
      Black. White.
            Red. My mark
scribbled in crayon.
          Defiant as the child refusing
ice cream.
         No, she says.
Whatever they offer, she wants
         something else, and she wants it
      now.

Spell for a Poet Getting On

May your hipbones never die.
May you hear the ruckus of mountains
in the Kansas of your age, and when
you go deaf, may you go wildly deaf.

May the neighbors arrive, bringing entire aviaries.
When the last of your hair is gone, may families
lovelier than you can guess colonize
the balds of your head.

May your thumbstick grow leaves.
May the nipples of your breasts drip wine.
And when, leaning into the grass, you watch
the inky sun vanish into the flat page

of the sea, may you join your lawn chair,
each of you content
that nothing is wise forever.

Spelunking

Our flames reach very short.
Only the thinnest of us pass
the squeeze. Dark is rising
up our legs. We are off the
map and cold. The one who
holds the clearest light is

Emily. We see the lengthening
fingers of rock, how water
makes its slow difference.
Her arm falls to her side.
The moving beam glistens
on Emily's white dress.

The Landscape of the Piano

is a winter. Snow stays on the plain but melts
off the hot backs of the mountains.

We travel. Ice is everywhere and there are temples
full of strange singing. We have caravanned, looking up.
We enter a wood and vanish into the grain.

*

In the heart of the piano, the strung back,
there is rain slanting down in glitters

and the air between the strands of rain
sings of Birth and Love and Death

and everything other: what we are.
But oh, say the skeptics, *How can it*

rain in a box? Until they open it, and
their faces stream with tears.

TWO

Matanzas

*Matanzas Beach, near St. Augustine, was named to com-
memorate Pedro Menendez' 1565 slaughter of Huguenot
settlers there. Menendez justified the murders by saying it
was not Frenchmen he had killed, but heretics.*

A rod jammed into the sand
the thin line from its tip to the sea
relaxed

and him down the beach
picking up broken angels' wings
with a boy's faith

in what swims in deep water
when suddenly, raptly, his rod bends
and he pounds towards it,

pounds heart-footed
towards what is silver and struggles
in every boy and

flushed, he reels it in.
What next, he never thought. It leaps
and gasps in his hands.

Django in Hang-Zhou

He is *waiguo ren*: foreigner. When he walks to
the market his dark head sees over theirs as if
he were a child, held on his father's shoulders.
They point at him and stare. He is twenty-one,
and empty as a thousand year-old wine jug.
He is also in love, not with what is foreign
in Hang-Zhou, but with what is most himself —
the cold and ancient lake, the blue mountains,
and, in spring, with the puffs of dust that followed
the galloping carts of emperors. I think he was
among the watchers who lined the streets when
these trees were small. I asked him once,
Why is it that Mandarin's so easy for you?
Because I'm a musician, he said, which was
like the doll, that still has many dolls inside.

Youth

For a student sitting under a noon tree

A bright band circles your wrist
because it has fallen off your hair
which, slippery as black water,
would not be stayed.

Outside the Library

The woman in the safari dress
takes out her glasses and
opens her book, the way a
watcher might use binoculars,
make of a limpkin picking at its
feathers, a rare and intimate
gift — she, who is forty-three
and learning about zygotes, she
whose handwriting has always
yearned too much for the left.
And she believes her cells are
orchids, which blossom and
divide more beautifully, now
that she knows they do. Which
is why she dresses in her dreams,
why she, all her life called mouse,
wears elephants.

At the Krystal

The black lady with the gold tooth
is crayoning in a map of Spain.
A thin purple rainbow has gathered
on the edge of her hand. *Francia,*
she has written where the map
falls off the page. Meanwhile,
rows of snapped pink rollers go
marching down her head towards
tonight, when Willie be stopping
by. But if Willie stood here now,
not even the name she stitched
under the red and yellow shell
on his shirt would tell her
who he was. She's traveling,
has passed over borders, is gone.

Dinner with Yun

Between us pasta cools, red as luck.
Your words cut the hungry air.
Yun, truth is the sweetest knife.
Let us never lie to one another.
Fry our tongues before we come to this!

Here, have a morsel dredged in crumb,
sauteed to a delicious gold. Have
the hors d'oeuvres of our hopeful marriages,
the men on our answering machines.
Take this wine.

The world through its thin glass rim can sing
if you rub it with a wet finger.

Decor

Franz and Marc live in New York white.
Even their Christmas trees
wear only white lights, white angels.
Their doorsills hoard no dust.
Their dresser tops are bare.
On one white wall, off-center,
hangs a face. Round holes
for eyes. Where the mouth
would be, perfectly smooth.

Deb wraps all in blue. Blue willow
for breakables. Blue quilt, blue
rug, blue lights. Otherwise, white
only, for how it looks against blue.
She longs for a man but says men
bode bad wind, like a bruised sky.
Deb is obsessed with sky.

I look for earth. Green and brown,
ecru for the clay women licked
on the beaches of South Carolina
because they lacked something
they could not name. Day after
day they returned, palms flat,
skirts spread wide, and one by
one, silent, ashamed of such need,
they'd rise and go home.

Breaking

for Lucinda

To stay alive, leave nothing whole. Crush a leaf.
Make it spill its green light.
       Jag a nail off its skin. Look through it.
It is the glittery nails of the dead that shine
   in rocks.
Open his smile and inside is rain which smokes like ice.
Even as you watch, his mouth, with its split smile
          begins to weep.

Tear a bedsheet in two and have
         two sheets.
Tear his letter in three
and three times he will tell you
that he loves you, but loves his small son more.
Tear the night sky in so many pieces
you cannot count them all.

You have lived.
I, he, she, they have lived.
Someone else will live,
     will find what you have scattered,
will pick the lost stars up
     like shy and tiny fish,
         will throw them back.

Six Ways

There are a thousand ways to play a staccato.
— Abby Simon, *Piano Quarterly*

i
Business

The beehived secretary's brisk heels
click across the polished floor.

ii
Play

Duck Duck Duck on straight or curly head.
GOOSE! Look how Amy chases Fred.

iii
Rendezvous

The silvery rain in the broad-brimmed hat
just lightly taps her fingers on the table.

iv
Obsession

The water in the kitchen will not stop dripping.
Purge me of his eyes.

v

Hunger

Each tap grabs a grub. The jackhammer
tears the street to pieces.

vi

Assassination

He was wondering over red or white roses. The barrage
comes so quickly it seems all one sound.

Keys

Whites lie like little coffins.

The black keys plot revolution,
the piano exploding into flowers
or suddenly disappearing in a spangly cloud.

They stand in their ranks.
Under their black coats their chests shine with gold.

The Prairie Woman Tells

He stared three twists of hay to ashes
vanished dolls burnt angels
eyes and hair and wings ashiver
before he spoke. Never, he said,
do you leave this place again.
The fists he made — two gleaming babies
thwacked on bone.

But o the young man
floating over the hill his yellow hair
astream and o his white robe
as we lay together on the crushed bluestem
on its flowery eyes and o Mary Mary Mary
he cried and then he flew,
Archangel of God he flew.

And Thorn fears the idiot wanderer
the Stengaard boy with his yellow hair
yes. But fears me more and so
makes this gift of dark blue skin
in token of what he does not understand:
the reason we came these thousand miles
why sat the go-down to break the sod
why with our two axes chopped it free
why with all his pumping we have no child.
I take the two jars to fill.
He lets me go. The grass blows light
green with the wind, but dark against.

---

go-down – a type of plow

THREE

Tuning the Felts

... Added to these problems is the matter of regulating the touch evenly, often caused by extensive moth damage to a piano action.
— Howard Chase, *Country Piano Tuner*

The soft grey lint, the dust,
and then they find the felts
and our voices begin to turn.
Oh we are tinny. How we shrill
as our treble loses bells.
How we thud in the bass, like
a man on uncarpeted stairs
in a house in the middle of the
night. We thought the moths,
like chance remarks, were
only small. We did not
notice how many they were.
We never imagined their hunger.

The Shoes

They were wine suede, with just a thin strap
across the ankle. Sometimes I could tell
they were wrong, but I didn't care.
I wore them with everything. When they began

to sag, it was only a little at first, like shoulders
at the end of the day, and it didn't matter that
my feet slid extra with each step. I pulled the strap
tighter. It bit a new hole. Then their color

turned sad and stains started to rise up their sides.
Water markings, the wavy outlines of tears. And
underneath how thin they grew, how easily
small stones would bruise. A heel came loose.

I nailed it back. But the nail head worked through
to my bare foot and every left step pained.
I took the shoes downtown. The aproned cobbler
turned one over, gave it back. *These are too far gone,*

he said. *Buy yourself some new shoes*, he said.
The sun hit the floor like new leather, hard and raw.

For

For the daffodil's horn that blazes spring   For the hooting taxis
that don't give a damn whose door they crunch   For the Levis
of New York City, out at the knees

For the shadows between hardwoods that hint of zebras   For
the zebra's yellow teeth that will bite if she can   For the way
her stripey neck can twist itself towards your arm   For other
beauties: the peacock and his unpleasant voice

For vivid violet lightning that won't stay put   For the sound
thunder makes after love, the bang that makes you jump
no matter how you steel, no matter how you want the flash
to be enough

For the jittery innocence under the skins of rivers the clear
way they skip over rocks as though the rocks' indigestibility
were of no importance   For the stones women swallow
when they marry   For the operation that removes the stones
so they can be kept as specimens or set in rings

For the way the birds do not realize they are flying   For
the baby who hums himself awake   For the cat in her
orange disregard   For the moment just before we understand
what the promised little talk is all about

35

Retreat

i

You crawl into the closet,
do not answer when I call.
My big husband,
huddled somewhere among
your darkened clothes,
I will send a shoe to find you,
send a shirt that knows your
shape, a necktie to catch
your throat and pull you out.

ii

There is laundry in the closet,
husband. There is laundry
we never dreamed. It is
heavy, damp, and dark.
It can take your breath away.

Message

Don't you see, there were limits
even to this, places where I could not
follow: into the heart of wood,
beyond the killing singing power line.

The Possibility of Suicide

That hot afternoon when your life shook
in the wire you tightened around your neck,
thin as electricity as I pulled it off and you
screamed at me *No!*
      there was something of insanity
in the way the crows called frantically, all
in one tree and would not fly though I stood
underneath, twisting the red wire in my hands.
And when you slept or did not sleep,
there was always the same prayer between us —
that you would not wake,
          the moment being gone
like a faithless pet, the steps having led
to the ceiling and stopped, that death
would come in the night to stroke
your veined forehead with gentle hands, easily,
not your fault, you could have been anything.

Against

Against gaud, the poet who slings words like drops of water
the way a dog shakes his fur, who slings so hard even fleas spin out
Against this: the dog who slings off all that is not-dog

Against dark, the reversion always to the easy choice, the one
dark glass every night always the dry, so careful never to choose
the sweet, what would they think

Against the unfaded rectangle of wall where I allowed the picture
too long, until it burned its image there, peach rising, moon-fuzz
over the lapping sea, and how shall I cover that space,
having no picture larger

Against the brain-coral, because it is no longer in the sea
and is a lie, because it gathers dust, my grandmother's body-dust
who died so many years before she died Against the black-red in me
my fury like an angry horse at her going to bed to wait

Against the rough and pitted stone, because I hold a carnelian
with its blood lights year after year, because I polish it
with a cloth whose emery wears my hands away,
because I passion this thing I do and you say
I should be satisfied, that I should not need you

Against my low and matted hair, my bitch-bones, against the food
I serve you raw, the fetching that I do Against you

Tickets to "The Crying Game"

*I stand at the edge, where the field of my life collapses into black
water. The things that live there have no eyes. I lean into air, and
as I fall I try to become a knife. I enter. I do not have breath
enough to touch bottom, not even with the tips of my hands. I
must swim now, or float until I die, the sky shrunken over me,
blue circle edged with rock.*

My eyes were not accustomed. Beside me not you, but a stranger,
whose hand strayed to my thigh like a mouse in the dark. "The
Crying Game" was in color, but I saw black and white. And shades
of grey. They say you can tell a good still by its gradations of
grey. I dream not in pictures but words, bright gold words with
wavy tails, swimming the fog of my sleep. Beside me someone's
touch, grey fingers finding a place as moist as the walls of caves
where the air has gathered like tears.

I have hidden in this pocket, just the narrow of my hand, what I
thought to throw away. I think I meant to find those stubs again,
to touch them with startle in my throat as when, on the screen,
fire shoots from his clenched fist and she collapses to the wall,
quick blood blooming from her opened neck, and the sky for us
both impossible in that dark.

When the Birds Sing

At dawn, before their wings can be told
from leaves, when light is still
a streak, like flying.

On dim days when all the fields go
veiled, and any named thing might be
something else.

Late, when a woman can no longer
take back what she has told
her man, they sing, and

she is alone, she thinks, in the barrens
of her heart, and yet she knows
the birds are there.

Gathering Roots for Tea

Sassafras, sweetgum, and scrub oak
struggle in needled sand. This
should be sea floor, and we fish.
I have wished for that, to fin
with no mind, musically through
the dark. But I am trying to
love what is, even pain, like
bright red berries that grow
low to the ground. And to expect,
on certain thin twigs, the yellow
clusters that say in their season,
Dig here. How like the stars are
the small round houses of sweetgums,
scattered everywhere in fall!

From the Closet

Tiny grey moths spangle the dark
as I lift the hangers down.
There are mouths in my skirts
beyond repair. Your jackets
swarm in ruined herringbone.
We knew, but we looked away.
We have nothing left to put on.

The shops are full, and all on sale.
You think new clothes can make us
young. History says you're wrong.
Yet open the door and step outside.
See how beautiful the patterns are.
No wonder the ancients gave them
names: Hunter, Balance, Lyre, Swan.

The Storm Flag

The dangerous flowers of cloud
stilled our slashing tongues.
We stuffed the jib, forced the
mainsail to the boom. You
fought the tiller. I played
both anchors out. Now half
the sky was black. A lashing
rain began and sent us down.
And our boat would not turn
into the wind, so we slapped
and rolled, sideways to the
swells. And drawers flew open,
snapped shut. And rain poured
in the porthole's eye, tight
enough for easy days. We wrung
out sopping towels and played at
gin, laying our discards straight
from the throat. And then the air
turned black, and the hairs
lifted on our arms and a light
slid down beside us. Nothing
we said, just light. And soon
around the boat the hard waves
began to calm and the moon
came out, and stars glittered
on the tips of the sea.

Nocturne

after Chopin

i

Drawing the oval across measure
lines, he thinks: *This Woman,*
and combs with his finger
her dark hair.
              The scent of
jasmine lingers on his hands.

ii

A warm wind splits the song
into two streams of birds,
each yearning south.
              He
lifts his pen, wanting to
stay their wings
              high above
the flowered islands.

iii

Somewhere he has left Helena,
trailing her fingers
              in the water.
He turns the pages.
The moon silvers the paper
where the notes sail,
              the small dark
notes with their flags,
the whole notes with none.

Kevin Plays the Goldberg Variations

A fleet of clouds crosses the skylight.
We are riding the wind of your hands.
Sometimes the jib runs easy in its white
curve. Sometimes we vibrate on little
speedy glitters, that build until we
slap through spray. Then fall,
and we settle on the swells like gulls
and the sea's so clear I want to cry.
We are far gone. Only you see the land,
that sweet, thin, dark edge, there where
for days we will feel ourselves rocking.

FOUR

Of

Of the angels   Of the parson made from the spinal bone of a horse
Of the parson's painted face, its eyes worn off and,
behind the cassock, the black painted wings

Of wings that swoop at dusk The turning bats diving for small stones
Of stones that fly of themselves when no one sees That soar
in flurries over grasslands and forest in search of ponds

Of someone's buttocks, smooth-skinned as river rock   And white,
because they have all these years kept secret Of the sudden white
someone's face turns, covered by hands, as the surgeon comes
sadly, stripping his mask

Of the mask of powder mother wears   Of the mask's red cheeks
its lipstick of Fatal Apple   Of the sparse black lashes of its eyes
Of the mask mother tilts upward to be kissed   Of her daughter,
whose heart sinks

Of what hangs folded behind the daughter's dresser to emerge
at night   Of what beats across the daughter's face no matter
that she shrouds herself in her sheets, pretending death
Of how the bats know otherwise.

That House

She wove notes into her braids.
Her mother did not notice.

She drew numbers on her fingerpads.
Her mother said, *Wash your hands.*

She curled strings into clefs.
They were gone when she came home.

She tried to sing with her fingers.
Her mother said *Stop that jittering.*

Her mother said *Look, you can't eat
pianos.* She said *Oh yes I can.* But

beets and roast and corn were set before
her. There was no music in that house.

Mommy, 1953

She scratches the soles of my new shoes with her knife. Now put them on, she says. I dream the linoleum is ice, that I hid those shoes and now I spin, my back arched deep, fast as a flower.

She gestures to the meat. My hands turn greasy, shaping bits of chopped cow. I wonder if death stops being dead if you cut it small enough. Clear the table, she says later. And don't stack the plates. I stiffen. My brother and sister play tiny violins.

She takes off her apron and leans over my bed. She knows how I look asleep. She knows how many roses there are on my night-gown. There is nothing I fear more than her dark red kiss.

Story

Once there was a girl, and her Mommy sent her away to Alaska, told her climb this mountain and be the first to get there, and you can come home again. But she didn't know how to climb mountains, and she didn't want to come home, so she stayed in the permafrost and watched the wildflowers open in summer, and in autumn she went north with the caribou and when they had their babies she would pull them out of the mothers and in a minute the babies would be able to eat grass and run away from the white following wolves. And she watched the Northern Lights, oh she did, and they made her think of the ones she made at school, scratching the black crayon off colors and how she used to get her fingernails so black with wax that even Mommy couldn't scrub them clean.

And the Mommy of this girl there once was, used to read the newspapers every day for news, how her daughter climbed that mountain, how she was the first. But the news never got printed and finally the Mommy gave up and got another daughter to take the place of the Alaska one, and she kept that daughter home and when the daughter grew up, she bought her a nice husband and a close house and at night she would go over and look in the windows to be sure the daughter was still there, and she was. And the Mommy was so happy.

The Discussion, 1958

Tonight you stuck my eyes with your fork.
I am writing this in the dark by feel
the way I used to draw pigs
with my eyes closed and their tails
always split from their bodies.
Dinner in this house begins
with stomachache, and ends
with slamming doors and I know
you've always wanted to do that.
And now you've done it. Congratulations.

Doctor, dinner started slowly
with a roast being carved by Daddy.
And the roast just lay there
and slices started to pile up on plates
and potatoes got put on and Mother
started so I could eat. But then
she wanted to know about school.
And I told her. But nothing is enough
for Mother. She wanted to draw
each moment out of me with a syringe,
and squeeze it empty and start again
until I had no blood left, but was just
bones in a bag. I'd tell her all I knew
but then she'd begin again. And again.
So then I said that she couldn't have me
and she said it was her right, the right
of family to own and love, and I said,
no, not own. And then she started

screaming and I screamed too and then
I said: *It's always like this. Can't you see*
why I hate to come home? And she said,
We aren't fighting, it's a discussion
a discussion a discussion. And then
she took her fork, and she pierced my eyes.
And I can't see any more, Doctor,
I can't see. And Daddy just sat there.

Daddy, 1959

Oh it's been so long since I talked to you,
our heads bent in the dusk together
when she was away.
And the weather's turned cold and wet
and it's dark by six
and when you get home I
don't see you, all those meetings
that own you, keep you gone.
So Sunday, let's walk to the top
of Mount Tam, and stop
at Mountain Home on the way
and call her to say we'll come
later. And then, Daddy, we can
stay all night, we can take a tent
and camp. And you can tell me
she doesn't mean it — all
those things she says — while
we're sleeping on the ridge
on the back of the Indian maiden
who jumped from these cliffs
for love, and whose hair
streams down the valley.

On the Train

On the train the bearded man
picks at his nails, looks down.

When I was twenty, I say, I
traversed Squaw Mountain on

the thin horses of skiis.
By noon I was buried to my waist.

Even the birds froze slowly.
Their claws broke. They fell.

And no one came, I tell him.
He picks at the dark crescent

between nail and skin.
He takes out a sandwich.

Around his lips mayonnaise
oozes its female cream.

The Deceptive Cadence

You make such lovely food, your mother says,
inspecting the peanut dip.

Such attractive people, your mother says
after the guests have gone.

And who was the young man with the beard?
Oh yes, the singer. Charming.

After the walk among the live oaks, dripping
moss like dancer's tulle,

she pronounces herself enchanted by the South,
by you, and this time

you know she has come around. Feeling warm,
you turn the page.

Passing Fifty

When I see a deer, innocent across the pasture,
                nuzzling its soft nose down,
it is always the same deer
                   I see, no matter that the deer
has died many times, its hide peeled from its bones,
    its face given to the ants,
                it is the same.

So why should I wake nights, suddenly
                  washed?
Why should my gown imitate my skin
      this way, so I have to get up and find
another, something cotton and dry,
    to start all over again
             this slow falling towards
     sleep?
Why do I keep seeing that deer
      night after night,
          stepping into evening grass?

Three for D'Arcy

1. Song for the Boyfriend

What did you spill this time?
The dirty little kings are shrieking again.
What have you spilled? *Her, her heart*
struggles for its life in the speedy water.

What did you lock up this time?
Your keys are shining like petted kittens.
Dark hang the dresses where I have closed her.
Darkly they flutter.

What skittered by you this time?
Never mind. She has gone among the flutes
where her long fingers can spell out,
white and wise, everything she learned from you.

2. In

In a jumpy wind that jitters your hair you flit from plan to plan
You are traveling hard with no map but your own blue veins:
on your thighs, on the insides of your arms, the gathering
arteries of traffic beginning to surge across your hands
So many roads, so many cities of blood.

In concerts you ragdoll, painted mouth pouring smoke, as
moment by moment your nights disappear but you are not
sorry and why should you be, having chosen these black walls,
this strobe-crossed dark no more hell you say than anyplace else
You strap your ankles and lean into air at the ends of cords
that may snap, and that they may is what you love.

You move in move out, your dozen boxes magic-markered
for the next time All those apartments all those men All
those books to be written which you begin and leave You
have left me behind, here where the dogwoods bald and
even the sweetgums are losing heart, here on my autumn
farm at my cluttered desk where I write my one story,
and yet, you know, there is joy in this. I have just realized
that the leaves have been throbbing all over, like a kissed girl,
enveloped by a lover, just before her clothes turn bright
and drift away.

3. How I Learned

For years I made you purple presents.
Mauve blouses, lavender skirts,
fuschia scarves that flowed.
For each occasion, another shade
of bruise, sweet as the fumes of
Daddy's disappearing Buick, achy as
the strokes of tight-lipped Mommy,
brushing my hair. I thought you'd
wear them. I thought they'd become
you, being blonde. But you put them,
all my purple gifts, in one deep drawer.
And now, grown, you take them out.
At first it pains, how new they are.
Then you smile. *Let's give these
away*, you say. And the spring sun
backlights your hair. You look
like some kind of angel, standing
there in your bedroom, the shine
of what to keep, and what to let go
falling through both our hands.

Beyond

Beyond the woman sitting over coffee, her tall books mountained
on formica, her papers scattered, new words – penciled over type –
crossed off, other words penciled in

Beyond anything she can say this cold morning   Beyond what
anyone can say, there are such pink swirls of cloud against
pale blue to make anyone sad that nothing lasts but yet becomes
something else also lovely or terrible   Beyond the imaginings
of the child in her midnight bed of a world beyond
her life when it will not matter that she lived

Beyond her high shelves of teddy bears, and the dolls she saw
through, even as they grinned behind their cellophane
and the child knew what was pretend and it was everything

even the pink clouds that melted to sugar on her lips even
her own body like a pruned tree which birds could flutter through
and her mother reach beyond, into her chest and out her back

Beyond her sheets of patterned cloth then paper
Beyond the penciled words like jet trails evanescing   Beyond
the place the jets were going when they turned to fire
as the woman looked out the window at the planes,
suddenly level with her eyes.

Under

Under a spreading sky, blue-pink as a wild egg,
a woman makes a bouquet of her life:
baby's breath, alyssum, sweet lobelia,
rosebuds of palest gold.
                            And she does this
not for bride's-sake but because the season
in the garden will spindle soon.
                            And also
because she wants this picture: herself,
hair dark as night before star-rise,
herself, proud in dirt-streaked jeans,
herself, flowers spilling from her arms.

About the Author

Lola Haskins' poetry has appeared in *Atlantic Monthly,
The Christian Science Monitor, The London Review of Books,
Prairie Schooner, Georgia Review, Southern Review, Beloit
Poetry Journal,* and *The Quarterly,* among others. She has
received awards from The Poetry Society of America, *The
New England Review/Breadloaf Quarterly, The Southern
Review, The New York Quarterly,* and *The Abiko Quarterly*
in Japan.

Besides writing poetry, Ms. Haskins enjoys translating it from
Spanish, as well as running, canoeing and playing the piano.
She has taught Computer Science at the University of Florida
since the late 1970s, and lives on a farm outside Gainesville
with her husband, Gerald, and assorted dogs, cats, ducks,
and peacocks.